D1211740

EXTREME MACHINES
IN SPACE

PATRICIA ARMENTROUT

The Rourke Press, Inc.
Vero Beach, Florida 32964

Patricia Armentrout specializes in nonfiction writing and has had several book series published for primary schools. She resides in Cincinnati with her husband and two children.

PHOTO CREDITS:
All photos © National Aeronautics Space Administration

EDITORIAL SERVICES:
Penworthy Learning Systems

Library of Congress Cataloging-in-Publication Data

Armentrout, Patricia, 1960-
    Extreme machines in space / Patricia Armentrout.
        p. cm. — (Extreme machines)
    Includes index.
    Summary: Describes various machines that have been used in outer space, including the space shuttle, Skylab space station, satellites, and unmanned space probes.
    ISBN 1-57103-214-2
    1. Space vehicles—Juvenile literature. [1. Space vehicles. 2. Outer space—Exploration.] I. Armentrout, Patricia. 1960- II. Title III. Series: Extreme machines.
TL793.A76 1998
629.47—dc21   98–24063
                                                              CIP
                                                              AC

Printed in the USA

TABLE OF CONTENTS

NASA AND MACHINES IN SPACE

Machines make space travel possible. Machines that travel in space are called spacecraft.

Some spacecraft are built to carry equipment that **transmits** (tranz MITS), or sends, information back to Earth. Some spacecraft are built to carry people.

National Aeronautics Space Administration (NASA) is the United States department that plans and launches space **missions** (MISH enz). This book will explore different kinds of spacecraft.

It takes special tools to repair extreme machines like the Hubble Space Telescope.

LUNAR ROVER

The 1969 Apollo 11 flight made history with the first moon landing. By Apollo 15, people were not only walking on the moon, they were driving on it too!

Astronaut Aldrin steps away from the lunar module Eagle.

Some astronauts get to have all the fun.

The lunar rover was a four-wheeled machine used on the moon. It had a television camera and antenna that gave the **astronauts** (AS truh nawts) direct contact with Earth. The rover traveled about 8 miles (12.8 kilometers) an hour and was powered by batteries. Astronauts stored rocks that they collected from the moon's surface in a bin behind the driver's seat.

SPACE SHUTTLE

The space shuttle is the first reusable spacecraft. A space shuttle is launched by two rockets. The shuttle reaches its **orbit** (AWR bit) at between 112 and 186 miles (180.32 and 299.46 kilometers) above the earth. Engines power the spacecraft while in orbit. A shuttle returns to Earth like a glider—without engine power.

A shuttle can carry a crew of seven astronauts as well as 65,000 pounds (29,500 kilograms) of cargo, called payload. The payload may be a **satellite** (SAT ul yte) or a **telescope** (TEL i SKOHP) that the shuttle places into Earth's orbit.

The space shuttle Columbia arrives at launch pad 39A at the Kennedy Space Center.

THE HUBBLE SPACE TELESCOPE

The Hubble Space Telescope (HST) orbits Earth. It is a huge telescope powered by the sun's rays. The Hubble has powerful camera lenses that take pictures of faraway objects.

The Hubble has made many important discoveries. Some of the pictures taken by Hubble include stars that are billions of miles away. A little closer to home, the Hubble has captured amazing photos of a **comet** (KAHM it) hitting Jupiter.

The Hubble Space Telescope takes pictures of objects billions of miles away.

SPACE STATION

A space station is a workshop in space. U.S. space station Skylab circled the Earth over 34,000 times during its mission. The Skylab crew observed the sun through telescopes and sent scientists on Earth thousands of pictures of the Earth's surface.

U.S. space station Skylab in Earth's orbit.

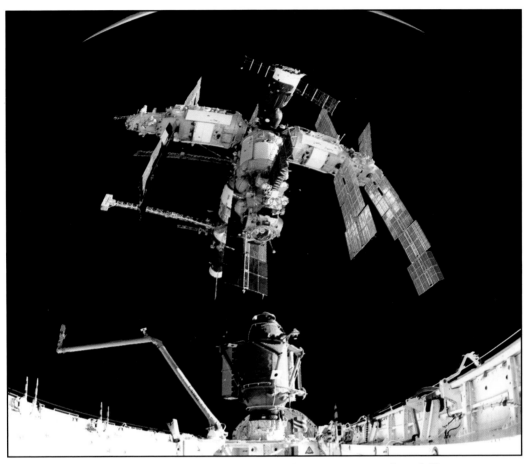

Huge solar panels help power the Russian space station Mir.

Russian space station Mir (MEER) is the first permanent space station. It has working, living, and docking areas. In 1995 Norman Thagard became the first American astronaut to board Mir. He stayed three months, studying in space.

SATELLITE

A satellite is an unmanned spacecraft that orbits Earth. Satellites have antennas and other instruments that are controlled by people on the ground.

Some satellites are used by weather forecasters. Other satellites are used for communication and send television and telephone signals all over the world.

Satellites are also used by the military. Some military satellites use cameras to observe enemy ground troops and equipment.

A satellite is released from the cargo bay of space shuttle Discovery.

UNMANNED SPACE PROBE

Probes are spacecraft that are sent to explore planets and their moons. Probes use television equipment to transmit pictures back to Earth. Some probes land on planets while other probes orbit the planets or moons.

Two probes were sent to explore the outer planets in 1977. Pictures were transmitted back to Earth. The pictures showed scientists six new moons that orbit Neptune and ten new moons around Uranus!

Space probe Magellan prepares for its long journey to planet Venus.

MISSION TO MARS

Mars, the fourth planet from the sun, has been explored by probes and machines called landers.

Pathfinder is a lander and a rover machine combined. It touched down on Mars on July 4, 1997.

The pathfinder rover traveled the Martian surface by remote control.

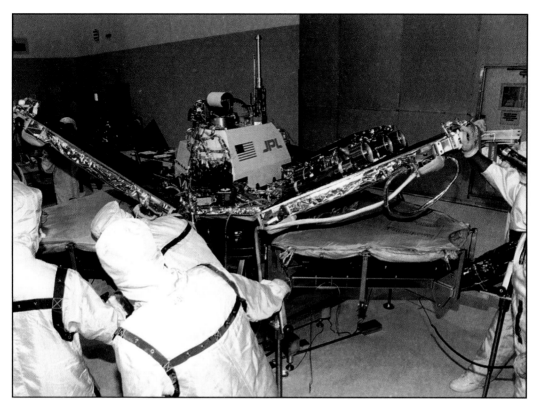

Scientists make final preparations to the Pathfinder lander and rover before its space journey to Mars.

Pathfinder was equipped with cameras, antennas, and other instruments that gathered information about Mars. The lander stayed in place, but the rover was able to move about the surface of Mars. The rover was controlled by an operator on Earth. Rover made news headlines as it explored the red planet.

A NEW SPACE STATION

The future of space travel begins with a new space station. Sixteen nations are working together to build and launch the International Space Station (ISS) to be completed in 2003.

The ISS will be used by men and women who will perform different jobs. Some people will study life science and others will work on medical research. Still other crew members will be trained to repair and maintain the space station.

The ISS will have docking ports for shuttles and also will be used to launch other spacecraft on new missions into outer space.

NASA uses computer drawings to show what the new space station will look like when it is completed.

GLOSSARY

astronauts (AS truh nawts) — people who travel in spacecraft

comet (KAHM it) — a mass of ice, frozen gases, and dust particles that travels around the sun

missions (MISH enz) — tasks or jobs

orbit (AWR bit) — a path that one object makes around another object, as in Earth's orbit around the sun

satellite (SAT ul yte) — a natural or man-made object in space that revolves around another object

telescope (TEL i SKOHP) — a tool used to view objects far away

transmits (tranz MITS) — sends information from one place to another

The Hubble Space Telescope uses big solar panels to absorb energy from the sun.

INDEX

FURTHER READING

Find out more about Extreme Machines with these helpful books and information site:

Berliner, Don. *Our Future In Space.* Lerner Publications Company, 1991.
Bendick, Jeanne. *Artificial Satellites Helpers in Space.* The Millbrook Press Inc., 1991.
Asimov, Issac. *Piloted Space Flights.* Gareth Stevens Publishing, 1990.
Internet address for NASA home page—http://www.nasa.gov/